THE MAGIC FLUTE

A CURTAIN-RAISER BOOK
The Magic Flute

by WOLFGANG AMADEUS MOZART

Pictures by RIERA ROJAS

FRANKLIN WATTS, INC.
575 Lexington Ave., New York, N.Y. 10022

This edition first published in the United States by
Franklin Watts, Inc., and in Great Britain by
J. M. Dent & Sons, Ltd., 1970
Illustrations copyright © 1970 Carl Ueberreuter Druck
und Verlag (M. Salzer), Wien
English text copyright © 1970 J. M. Dent & Sons Ltd.
and Franklin Watts, Inc.
Quotations from Edward J. Dent's English version
of the libretto of *The Magic Flute* by permission of
Oxford University Press
Designed and produced by Carl Ueberreuter Verlag, Vienna
Library of Congress Catalog Card Number: 70-106160
SBN 531-01929-2
Printed in Austria

Mozart and *THE MAGIC FLUTE*

Wolfgang Amadeus Mozart, the brightest star ever to appear in the musical firmament, was the youngest of the seven children of Leopold Mozart, a musician attached to the archiepiscopal court in Salzburg. From his mother, Anna Marie Pertl, young Mozart inherited a happy temperament and a passionate love of the theatre, from his father his musical gifts; for Mozart senior, son of an Augsburg bookbinder, was an excellent violinist and minor composer. It was he who gave little Wolfgang his first lessons and with feelings of love and ambition watched over the development of his extraordinary talent.

Many amazing tales are told of the musical child prodigy. When only four he was able to play his first little piano pieces faultlessly, drew notes for a piano concerto on paper and played the violin in the family chamber orchestra without having learnt at all. When he was six he performed with his sister Nannerl before the emperor's family in Vienna, leaped onto Maria Theresa's lap, put his arms round the empress and kissed her, promised to marry Marie Antoinette (later the unhappy Queen of France) and in his high, childish voice, quite unabashed, criticized the piano playing of Joseph, who later became emperor. Far from taking offence, Joseph commissioned an opera from him when Mozart came back to Vienna at the age of twelve. The performance of the charming little work *La finta semplice* had to be put off, so it fell to the Viennese doctor Anton Mesmer to stand godparent at Mozart's theatrical baptism when his first operetta *Bastien and Bastienne* was performed in the doctor's Garden theatre.

Ten years later Joseph II opened his "Nationalsingspiel" in the old Hofburg theatre in Vienna, the purpose of the enlightened emperor being to give his people opera in their own language. The highest achievement of this short-lived imperial enterprise was Mozart's opera *Die Entführung aus dem Serail (The Abduction from the Seraglio)* which reached the stage of the Hofburg theatre at last in 1782 after endless intrigue. It was Mozart's wedding song and the birth of German opera, no less. Later in 1787 Goethe summed things up by saying in a letter to a friend: "All our efforts to confine ourselves to what is simple and on a small scale went for nothing when Mozart came on the scene. *Die Entführung aus dem Serail* put all to rout." But the "Nationalsingspiel" which had opened with such high hopes had to close its doors, and so Mozart was obliged to write the texts of his other operas in Italian. With the triumphant first performance of *Le Nozze di Figaro (The Marriage of Figaro)* at the Hofburg theatre in 1786 Mozart reached the peak of his Viennese good fortune. After that he was dropped and quickly forgotten. The farther he departed from the fashionable forms of composition, the more isolated he became.

Thus it came about that *Don Giovanni* was given its first performance in 1787 not in Vienna but in Prague; that in 1790 the premiere of *Cosi fan tutte* in the Hofburg theatre was rather poorly received; and that finally Mozart found himself in desperate straits for lack of money. Yet from amid all this anxiety and harassment bloomed the miraculous *Magic Flute*. But Mozart's days were already shadowed by death. This last opera he had composed not for the courtly Burgtheater but for the popular Freihaustheater belonging to his friend and librettist Emanuel Schikaneder who collaborated closely with him and who, indeed, wrote the part of the gay bird-catcher, Papageno, for himself. When the show opened on the 30th September 1791 he played Papageno and Mozart himself conducted, "out of respect for a gracious public worthy of honour and out of friendship for the author of the work," to quote from the playbill. The opera was an immense success, but within two months Mozart had died. He had worked tirelessly on his *Requiem* until the last. Indeed, in all his short life he had served his genius faithfully, never writing without the utmost care or failing to use to the full his truly miraculous gifts.

Long, long ago, when the world was still ruled by supreme beings with magic powers, in a distant corner of the earth lay the kingdom of the Queen of the Night. A great, gloomy forest surrounded her temple and hid it from all men's eyes.

The queen had a vain and arrogant nature. It was not enough for her to rule over night and darkness. She wanted to make the Kingdom of Sun and Light subject to her as well, and spent her days and nights plotting to increase her power. When she sat on her throne of stars, over which the silver crescent of the moon blazed like a diamond, its glittering light seemed far too dim. For both the moon and the stars faded in the light of the sun. The Kingdom of Light was governed by a wise man called Sarastro. His nature was as pure and noble as the queen's was dark and evil. Vanity and lust for power were alien to his heart. He loved mankind and wanted to lead them to freedom and harmony. But as long as the Queen of the Night was plotting mischievously, his kingdom was threatened with downfall. So Sarastro made a wise and careful plan.

The Queen of the Night had a most beautiful daughter, whose name was Pamina. Her beauty outshone the light of the moon, her hair gleamed golden as starlight and her eyes were as black as the velvet black of the night sky. Her heart was so true and pure that even the evil spirit of her mother had no power over her.

Sarastro planned to kidnap Pamina and bring the Queen of the Night to repentance by this just punishment. One night, Sarastro's servants forced their way into the temple, seized the beautiful girl and brought her to their master.

The Queen of the Night was inconsolable at the loss of her beloved daughter. But in her pride she had no thought of remorse. She swore a terrible vengeance on Sarastro that would end in his downfall.

But how was she to regain Pamina? Her evil sorcery was powerless against Sarastro's purity. Faithful servants guarded his palace and the Queen of the Night could never, never gain admission to his sun temple.

For many nights the queen sat on her throne of stars and pondered. No one was allowed to disturb her, not even her most trusted attendants, three magical ladies. Now her plan was complete...

At that time there lived in a mighty kingdom a handsome young prince named Tamino. He liked nothing better than to go hunting and to rove through the woods. Sometimes he would not return home for several days.

He would sleep under the wide canopy of trees, waking at dawn with the song of the birds, watching the animals and losing all sense of time.

One day Tamino was tracking a magnificent deer which he intended to kill. The prince penetrated deeper and deeper into the forest, but the deer seemed to be eluding him. He glimpsed its mighty antlers, now here, now there, between the tree trunks, but next moment they had vanished again. Tamino ran this way and that until he lost all sense of direction. The forest was growing more and more dense, and soon Tamino became apprehensive. He felt as though he had wandered into an enchanted forest which would never let him go.

Suddenly a huge snake reared up before Tamino and hissed angrily at him with its poisonous breath. The prince started back

in terror. He called for help but no one heard him. No matter how fast he ran, the snake pursued him.

Suddenly the trees cleared and Tamino saw a temple standing at the foot of some huge crags. But just as he thought he was safe, Tamino heard the snake hiss again, very close to him. He turned and saw the monstrous creature coiled to strike. The prince was so exhausted and so terrified that he fell unconscious.

This was the moment the Queen of the Night had been waiting for. For it was she who had enticed Tamino to this place with her cunning power.

No sooner had the prince sunk senseless to the ground, than the door of the temple opened and the queen's three attendants

stepped out, each with a silver spear in her hand. Their faces were veiled so that no one could tell whether they were beautiful or hideously ugly.

"Die, monster, by our power!" all three cried together. They flashed their silver spears and pierced the snake. Fatally wounded, it writhed on the grass.

Now the three ladies looked at the unconscious prince at their feet, and their delight was unbounded.

"What a beautiful youth! How tender his face in sleep, how pure his brow, how noble his mouth!" they said, and each of the three ladies thought: Yes, he is beautiful enough for me to love. But they kept their thoughts to themselves, because for so long as they served the Queen of the Night they had to reject the world of men and keep love from their hearts. So they veiled their faces when they showed themselves outside the temple. And the handsome young prince, as they well knew, was destined for a higher task.

"He will defeat Sarastro and restore Pamina to the arms of her mother," said the first lady.

"Go, give the queen the good news! I will stay here," said the second.

"No, *I* will stay here," retorted the third.

"No, I!" all three now cried together. Each of them wanted to watch over Tamino and none was prepared to yield. So all they could do was to leave their charge alone and unguarded.

Together the three ladies entered the temple once more.

The Queen of the Night also had a manservant, a cheerful fellow whose name was Papageno. He was the royal bird-catcher and jester and he looked both his parts, for he wore a garment entirely made of bright feathers. He looked more like a strange, big bird than a man. Papageno roamed about the forest all day, calling on his flute to the most beautiful of the birds and catching them for the Queen of the Night.

Papageno came out of the forest at the very moment when Tamino awoke. The prince looked about him in amazement, for he did not at first know where he was. Then he caught sight of the dead snake.

"Thank heavens!" Tamino cried. "I am alive and the monster is dead! Who has saved me? To whom do I owe this happy fate?"

Suddenly Tamino heard a cheerful melody on the flute and then a man's voice. Papageno appeared, with his bird ladder on his back. The feathers of his garment flicked up and down as he made a few awkward dancing steps, singing:
"I am the bird-catcher, am I
So jolly, hi-di, ho-di-hi!"

It almost looked as if he were trying to fly, although his wings would surely have been too short. He was so comic that Tamino had to laugh aloud.

"Hoy there!" he called to the strange apparition.

"What do you mean, 'hoy there'?" asked Papageno, feeling deeply offended.

"Tell me, my jolly friend, who are you?"

"Who am I? Foolish question! I'm a man, like you." Papageno cast a suspicious glance at Tamino's grand clothes. Although he knew nothing of the world beyond the forest, the temple, the humble straw hut in which he lived and the attendants of the Queen of the Night, still Papageno realized that the strange youth was no ordinary man. He did not feel quite at ease when he asked: "But tell me, who are you?"

"I am a prince, and my name is Tamino. My father is a king and rules over many countries and people."

Since Tamino was pleasant and not at all haughty, Papageno grew more confident. He made a little bow to the prince and put his flute to his lips again.

"Now tell me one thing," said the prince, when Papageno had finished. "Where are we, and what are you doing in this place?"

"Have you not heard of the Nightly Star-blazing Queen?" Papageno answered mysteriously.

"The Nightly Star-blazing Queen — do you mean the great Queen of the Night, of whom my father has so often told me?" asked Tamino in surprise.

"Good guess!" said Papageno, proud that he could swagger now and instruct the prince. "There is her temple. No man has yet seen the Star-blazing Queen. I catch the prettiest birds for her, and for that her servants give me food and drink... You would not believe how they tremble before me," he whispered. "I have the powers of a giant." He drew himself up until the feathers of his garment stood on end.

13

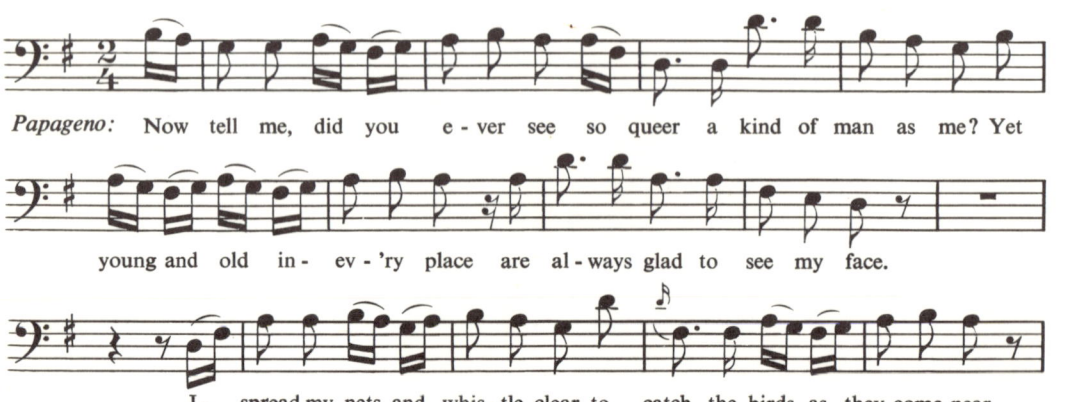

Papageno: Now tell me, did you ever see so queer a kind of man as me? Yet young and old in ev-'ry place are al-ways glad to see my face. I spread my nets and whis-tle clear to catch the birds as they come near.

"Then it was really you — the brave man who slew that poisonous snake over there?"

Now Papageno noticed the dead snake for the first time.

Shuddering, he drew back a step, too frightened to speak a word. Tamino took his silence for modesty.

"Thank you, my valiant friend!" cried the prince, much moved. "Do not reject my thanks! But tell me how you killed the monster? You have no weapons."

Papageno grew hot under his feathery robes. But suddenly he found his tongue, and his courage, again.

"Oh, it was nothing," he replied, as carelessly as possible. "*I* need no weapons. One strong squeeze of the hand is enough." But he was thinking to himself: I have never been as strong as that in my life!

"Papageno!" came a voice from the temple at that moment. The three veiled ladies had come out again and were shaking their fists at the liar. Papageno looked down dejectedly. But his remorse did him no good. One of the ladies stepped up to him and fastened a golden padlock on his mouth, so that he could not speak another word. This was torture to such a chatterbox.

"H'm, h'm," he grunted, looking so crushed and miserable that the prince felt truly sorry for him.

But now the three ladies turned to Tamino.

"Greetings, noble youth!" they said. "Welcome to the kingdom of the Queen of the Night!"

Tamino bowed respectfully.

"We saved you from this snake," one of the ladies continued. She drew a portrait from the folds of her robe and handed it to the prince. "This painting is sent to you by the great queen. It is a portrait of her daughter Pamina. If you find that this face appeals to you greatly, then you are sure of glory, fame and happiness."

Tamino looked at the picture and was at once delighted with the enchanting maiden looking out at him. The prince had never seen such a lovely face before. His heart was suddenly on fire with love. He sang Pamina's praises in tender words and his only desire was to win her for himself.

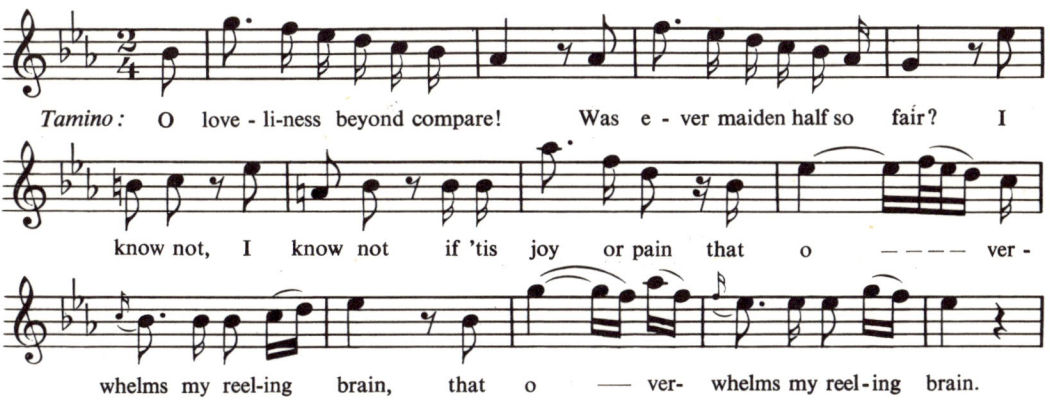

Tamino: O love-li-ness beyond compare! Was e-ver maiden half so fair? I know not, I know not if 'tis joy or pain that o- - - - -ver-whelms my reel-ing brain, that o - - ver- whelms my reel-ing brain.

The three ladies told Tamino of Pamina's abduction, Sarastro's cunning and the sufferings of the inconsolable mother, the Queen of the Night.

"I will rescue Pamina from Sarastro's power!" cried the prince. "The villain shall fall! Long live the mighty queen!"

At that moment there was a terrible clap of thunder. The sky darkened, the crags parted, and in the brilliant light of the stars the Queen of the Night appeared. Her cold, unapproachable

17

beauty made Tamino shiver. How exalted and strange she seemed to him, surrounded by a blaze of stars! In vain he tried to see some resemblance in her features to Pamina's gentle charm.

"Do not tremble, my dear son," the Queen began in bewitching tone. "You alone can fill a troubled mother's heart with new hope. You are of noble birth, innocent and valiant. Pamina is worthy of you, as of no other. Follow the voice of your heart, then you will conquer Sarastro and give me back my child! If you release Pamina, she is yours forever."

When she had finished, the Queen of the Night vanished as suddenly as she had appeared. The stars faded, the rocks resumed their places and Tamino was left alone with the three ladies and Papageno.

Before the prince had recovered from his astonishment, the first lady came up to him and handed him a golden flute.

"A gift from our Queen — take it," she said. "This is a magic flute, which will protect you wherever you go, and keep you from misfortune."

The second lady at last took pity on the wretched Papageno, who was distressed because he could not even move his tongue. The lady took the golden padlock from his mouth and handed him a silver glockenspiel instead.

"The Queen forgives you," she said. "So chatter on, but remember always that lies have crooked legs!"

Then all three ladies said together:

"The magic flute and these silver bells will lead you safely to Sarastro's kingdom. Three boys will be your guides."

"Wait! Stop!" Papageno interrupted in dismay. "What has all this to do with me? I have no wish to travel."

"The Queen commands you to accompany Tamino! The prince will protect you, and in return you are to be his servant!"

With that, the three ladies returned to the temple.

Papageno was not at all delighted to have such a privilege con-

ferred on him. To tell the truth, he was not exactly brave, and preferred to perform his heroic deeds with his tongue. He went on grumbling as he prepared to follow Tamino. But he did know his way through the forest well, and without him Tamino would never have found Sarastro, for the three boys who were to serve them as guides did not appear.

The journey lasted many days and Tamino was burning with impatience to see Pamina.

"Are you sure we have not lost our way?" he asked Papageno repeatedly.

"As certain as that I am a man and not a bird," Papageno answered again and again. When Tamino shook his head doubtfully the bird-catcher became offended and went on ahead, refusing to speak to the prince.

And that was how Papageno arrived at Sarastro's palace before Tamino. There he began to feel uneasy and kept glancing nervously around him.

But Papageno's curiosity was almost greater than his fear. He crept softly from one window of the palace to another, peeping cautiously inside. There he saw the most splendid rooms, the richest furniture and carpets; gold and ivory gleamed, silvery glasses and costly silks shimmered. But when Papageno reached the last window he almost fainted with terror. A terrifying, dark and frowning face looked out at him, rolling its eyes wildly and gnashing its white teeth.

This was Monostatos, Sarastro's Moorish slave, who guarded the lovely Pamina.

Monostatos was as frightened by Papageno as the bird-catcher had been by the Moor, for Monostatos had never before seen such a strange creature as the gaily feathered Papageno. When Papageno rang his silver glockenspiel, the Moor was seized with panic and fled in terror.

Papageno summoned all his courage and entered the palace. It did not take him long to find Pamina, for he could hear her heartbreaking sobs through the door.

Pamina did not know why Sarastro had kidnapped her. She was longing for her mother and had no idea of the evil powers of the Queen of the Night. The girl could not understand why Sarastro was always kind and friendly toward her and yet held her an

innocent prisoner. Nevertheless, Pamina would have endured all this patiently, had it not been for Monostatos. She feared the Moorish slave with his ugly face, who never let her out of his sight day and night.

So when the door opened and, instead of Monostatos' grin, Papageno's good-natured face appeared, Pamina dropped her handkerchief in astonishment. Papageno picked it up and handed it to her with such a comical bow that Pamina had to smile, although the tears were still running down her cheeks.

"Who are you and where have you come from?" she asked.

"I am Papageno, bird-catcher to your mother, the mighty Queen of the Night," Papageno answered proudly. "I have come to free you from your imprisonment. That is," he interrupted himself hastily, "the two of us have come. The other one will be here in a moment. He is a prince and his name is Tamino."

"A prince?" exclaimed Pamina in surprise. "Tell me what all this means!"

"It is simple," said Papageno. "Your mother, the Star-blazing Queen of the Night, has devised the most cunning plan in the world. She has shown the handsome young prince your portrait and now he is burning with love for you and the determination to free you."

"He loves me? Oh, how wonderful!" Pamina almost embraced Papageno in her joy. "But what is the matter with you? You seem so sad!"

"Ah!" Papageno sighed. "Soon you will have your Tamino and Tamino will soon have his Pamina... But who will I have? It makes me want to tear out all my feathers when I think that Papageno does not have a Papagena."

"Poor Papageno!" said Pamina gently. "You have a good heart and look so sweet and funny in your bright feathers. You are sure to find a girl soon who will love you, one you can call your very own Papagena, perhaps sooner than you think. But tell me, where is Tamino now?"

"That is the trouble," replied Papageno. "Your mother's servants told us that three boys would guide us, but we have not seen them yet. It seemed silly to stop and look for the three boys,

so I went on ahead. Now that I have found you, come with me please, Pamina, as we must escape from here quickly!"

Meanwhile, Tamino had walked on alone. Although he did not know the way, he was not afraid of the dark forest. The prince trusted in his magic flute and his love for Pamina; surely both would lead him to his goal. Gradually, he became less impatient, his thoughts were calmer, and he felt quite at peace.

Suddenly the forest lightened, and rays of sunlight fell across the path and played on the treetrunks. Surrounded by brilliant light, three boys stood before Tamino, each with a silver palm twig in his hand.

"You are moving toward your goal, Prince," they said, "but hard trials await you, which only a strong man can survive. Be resolute, patient and silent! If you follow our advice you will win through to the end!"

Before Tamino could answer, the three boys had disappeared again. While the prince was still reflecting on the mysterious meaning of their words he saw a grand, pillared temple standing in a green meadow. Over the door the words TEMPLE OF WISDOM were written, in great golden letters.

Tamino approached the temple and would have entered, but a priest barred his way. "What do you seek in this holy temple, stranger?" he asked.

"A girl, pure and innocent as the morning and beautiful as the day, who has been taken prisoner by the villainous Sarastro."

"Taken from the darkness of night, you mean," answered the priest. "The complaints and false words of the Queen of the Night have poisoned you. As long as hatred and revenge guide you, Pamina will remain lost to you. Sarastro is no villain. His wisdom is infinite and no ignorant man will be admitted to his sanctuary."

The door of the temple closed behind the priest and Tamino

TEMPLE OF WISDOM

was left alone, wondering and thoughtful. What was he to make of all this? Who spoke the truth, the Queen or the priest?

Heavy-hearted, the prince sat down on the grass and began to play his magic flute. As he did so, the animals crept out of the woods: bear, wolf and fox, deer and stag, hare and squirrel; even the beetles crawled out of their holes in the ground. Not one of them harmed another. They all listened reverently to the beautiful music. The birds fell silent, for the music of the flute was far lovelier than their own song.

When Tamino stopped playing the animals returned, one after another, to the forest. Whistling and twittering, the birds rose into the air.

In the distance Tamino suddenly heard another tune on a flute which he knew well. That could only be Papageno! The prince hurried toward the sound, but the echo had deceived him. Just as Tamino was entering the forest, Papageno and Pamina were approaching the temple from the palace, pursued by Monostatos.

The Moor had discovered their flight, and because Pamina could not run fast enough he had finally overtaken them.

Pamina fell exhausted on the grass. "All hope is lost!" she cried, and burst into tears.

Then Papageno began to play on his silver glockenspiel, and suddenly Monostatos began to hop and twist. He danced into the forest, singing in his deep voice:

"That tune is so jolly, that tune is so sweet!
Tra-la-la, tra-la-la!"

Monostatos: O-listen, what is it that tinkles so clear? La-ra-la la la la-ra-la, la la la-ra-la! 'Tis something I never did see nor did hear. La-ra-la la la la-ra-la la la, la-ra-la!

Pamina sighed her relief, but scarcely had Monostatos disappeared into the forest when a loud fanfare of trumpets sounded. This fanfare announced the approach of Sarastro. A splendid procession, like a king's train, was moving toward the temple.

"Long live Sarastro!" shouted the priests and subjects of the Lord of Wisdom and Light.

At the last came Sarastro himself, commanding respect and obedience by his stately bearing.

Pamina and Papageno clutched each other's hands, trembling. But as soon as the girl had seen Sarastro she ran to him and flung herself weeping at his feet.

"Stand up," said Sarastro kindly. "You have done nothing wrong. It is only through ignorance that you have set yourself against my law."

At that moment Tamino came out of the forest, led by Monostatos. The Moor was grinning maliciously. He could not have hoped for a better catch.

Although many people were gathered in the square before the temple, the prince at once found Pamina among them. Tearing himself free from Monostatos, he ran to her side.

"Pamina!"

"Tamino!"

They embraced as though they had always known each other. Sarastro parted them gently. "Tamino, you are not yet worthy to make Pamina your own," he began gravely. "First prove that your heart is pure and that you have not been dazzled by the dark power of the Queen of the Night. Only then may Pamina be truly yours."

"What must I do to prove it?" asked Tamino.

"Strive for wisdom and be steadfast and silent," Sarastro replied. "A priest will conduct you and your fine-feathered companion to my temple of ordeal. Obey all the advice he gives you. Isis and Osiris, the gods of wisdom, will watch over your every step." He took away Tamino's magic flute and Papageno's silver glockenspiel. "And now, farewell!"

A priest opened the door of the temple and before Papageno and Tamino knew what was happening, they were pushed inside and sacks pulled over their heads, so that they could no longer see anything. They could only hear the door closing behind them. Then they were engulfed in total silence and darkness.

Tamino walked on, reflecting in silence, but Papageno began to whimper pitifully. Muffled thunder rolled in the distance and made the frightened creature shake still more.

By the time priests at last removed the sacks, an eternity

seemed to have passed. Now they found themselves in a courtyard surrounded by high pillars.

"We are in the forecourt of the temple," the priest told them. "Prince, are you prepared to submit yourself to all our tests? Are you prepared to give your life to win the girl you love?"

"Yes," Tamino answered firmly.

"But what have *I* got to do with this?" asked Papageno miserably. "I'm quite happy with what I have. That is," he added, "I would so much like to have a pretty, merry girl of my very own. But I will certainly not find her here."

"You will find her if you pass the test," the priest responded.

"Is that really true?" asked Papageno doubtfully. "What will she look like, this girl?"

"Just like you," answered the priest.

"Like *me*?"

"Yes, like a gay, bright bird, and her name is Papagena."

"Pa-pa-ge-na!"

"If you want to win her," the priest continued, "follow me into the Temple of Ordeal. Are you ready?"

Papageno nodded, but he was not really happy about it.

"And now, hear Sarastro's command," said the priest solemnly.

"Keep silent, whatever happens. Silence is our highest duty in this place. Take no notice of strange voices, and do not listen to women's pleading. One word too many and your happiness will disappear."

Having given these instructions, the priest went away and left Tamino and Papageno alone.

Once again dull thunder rolled heavily in the distance, the sun darkened and soon black night was all about them.

"Tamino, where are you?" cried Papageno fearfully.

"Be quiet and think of your Papagena!" the prince warned him.

"Ah, she'll have to look for someone else! I have had enough of all this magic. If only I were outside again!"

As if to punish Papageno's babbling, a jagged flash of lightning split the sky, followed by a rumble of thunder. Now, in the lightning flash, Tamino and Papageno saw that the three veiled ladies of the Queen of the Night were with them.

"You are lost! Sarastro plans your ruin. Follow us, or you will not get out of here alive!" cried the three ladies.

"I knew it," said Papageno to Tamino. "But you would not listen to me."

"Shh!" said Tamino, behaving as if he had neither seen nor heard the ladies.

Once again lightning split the darkness for an instant, and now the three ladies had vanished.

"Alas!" whimpered Papageno. "Now they have gone, and our last hour has struck."

But Tamino had no doubt that the appearance of the three ladies was only the first part of the test. Naturally the Queen of the Night had sent her messengers to tempt him, he thought. If I had listened to their chatter and broken my silence everything would already be lost.

Tamino was right. The Queen of the Night could scarcely contain her rage when the three ladies returned, having achieved nothing. For if Tamino were steadfast, Pamina would be lost to her forever.

Once again the Queen of the Night sat on her throne of stars and pondered. When the moon and stars faded and morning dawned she had devised another clever plan. Pamina herself must force the prince to break his vow. Tamino would certainly not be able to withstand her pleas.

The Queen of the Night cast her most powerful spell and appeared magically at her daughter's side. The beautiful Pamina was in a charming garden, close to Sarastro's palace. She lay asleep in a bower, surrounded by roses. The garden was a carpet of flowers, fragrant with a thousand blooms. Rare and extraordinary birds perched in the branches of the trees, preening their brilliant feathers.

Monostatos the Moor was jealously guarding the sleeping girl. He watched Pamina with lovelorn eyes. Since Sarastro had set him to guard Pamina, Monostatos had been falling more und more in love with the beautiful maiden. The fact that Pamina would have nothing to do with him — that he filled her with fear and disgust — both troubled and enraged him.

Ah, if I could steal a single kiss from her! he thought. She is asleep and surely won't notice . . . Yes, I'll risk it!

Monostatos stooped over the sleeping Pamina. But as his shadow fell over her face, she awoke and screamed in horror as she saw the Moor's face so close to her own. Monostatos rushed off in alarm and hid behind a tree.

At that moment there was a mighty crash of thunder, the earth opened and the Queen of the Night appeared.

"Mother!" cried Pamina. "Dearest mother! Have you come to protect me from the Moor, or can I flee with you from this place which is so full of terrors for me?"

"I cannot protect you, my child, or take you from here, for Sarastro's power is greater than mine. But I have come to give you some good advice. Tamino, whom you love, is doomed eternally unless you can persuade him to escape. Look for him! Hurry! Warn him of Sarastro's sinister plans. You see this dagger in my hand? You are to kill Sarastro with it. If you do not, my kingdom will fall into his power. Decide between him and me, your mother."

When the Queen of the Night had spoken, the power of her spell was over. She had to sink back into the earth and return to her temple. The ground closed over her, and Pamina was once again alone.

She stared aghast at the dagger her mother had left behind. "I can never kill Sarastro," Pamina said to herself. "Sarastro is so good, and my mother plans a dreadful revenge. What shall I do? And where shall I find Tamino?"

Monostatos had heard everything from behind his tree. He ventured out again and approached Pamina, smirking scornfully. He could not forgive her revulsion for him. And now Monostatos saw a chance to revenge himself.

"Now, my fair beauty, what is going on in your pretty little head?" he asked spitefully. "Is the dagger already burning your fingers? Do you know that you are in my hands? If I tell Sarastro your plans for vengeance, you and your mother are both lost. What do you say to that, my sweet little dove?"

Neither the Moor nor Pamina had noticed Sarastro's arrival.

Sarastro: We know no thought of— ven-geance with-in these tem-ple-walls-, where love leads back to— du-ty who-e'er from du-ty- falls; by friendship's kind-ly— hand— held fast, he finds the land of— light — — — at last.

"In this place vengeance is unknown," he said calmly. "I know, Pamina, that your mother's evil spirit has no power over you. Put your trust in the wisdom of the gods, then your happiness and Tamino's will be fulfilled. Monostatos, leave this place and never let me set eyes on you again!"

Monostatos obeyed and ran away. But in his heart he swore vengeance. I will go to the Queen of the Night, he thought, then we shall see who is stronger, she or Sarastro.

Pamina thanked Sarastro for his graciousness and promised to obey his advice. But she was too young to understand fully, and also, she was in love! She could not help thinking sorrowfully of Tamino all the time. And in the end she could bear the uncertainty of her fate no longer and set out in search of him.

Until now Tamino had withstood all his ordeals like a man, in contrast to the talkative Papageno, who was unable to hold his tongue. The prince reflected on all his experiences since he had entered Sarastro's kingdom. And in the end he began to understand Sarastro's wisdom and the meaning of the tests. Now, too, he understood the words of the three boys and the priest's warning. But the time of trial was not yet over and the hardest test still lay ahead of the prince.

Next Tamino and Papageno came to a wide, bright hall. Here they found food and drink on an immense table; since entering the temple Tamino and Papageno had not had anything to eat and they had now been journeying for a long time.

For the second time Tamino saw the three boys. Smiling, they handed the magic flute to him and the glockenspiel to Papageno. Sarastro had taken both from them at the temple, but now he was returning their flute and bells.

"Strengthen yourselves with food and drink," said the three boys. "You are not yet at your goal. Courage, Tamino, and you, Papageno, keep silence!"

This time Papageno obeyed. Scarcely had the three boys vanished again when he began to eat voraciously and had no more time for chattering.

Tamino was not interested in the table laden with food. He sat down on a grassy bank near by, and played on his golden flute. Suddenly he heard Pamina's voice calling his name.

Guided invisibly by Sarastro's power, the maiden had reached this place in her search for Tamino. She did not know that she herself was now setting her beloved the hardest test of all.

Following the sound of the magic flute, Pamina called Tamino's name again and again as she ran down one dark corridor after another. Then at last, between two marble pillars, she caught a glimpse of Papageno's bright feathers and immediately afterwards she saw Tamino. She rushed toward him joyfully.

But Tamino behaved as if he had not seen her and went on playing his flute.

"Tamino!" cried Pamina, "are you not glad to see me? I was so afraid, I *had* to look for you! Now that I have found you, everything will be all right . . ."

"Your Tamino is overcome with melancholy," said Papageno, shaking his head sadly. "He has not spoken a word to me for days. I am very glad that you have come, for I am bored to death."

"Tamino!" Pamina cried again. "Look at me! Won't you have anything more to do with your Pamina?"

But it was no use. Tamino did not look at her once.

"Farewell, then!" cried Pamina. "If you no longer love me I do not wish to live! My mother is angry with me and plans revenge.

And Sarastro, whom I trusted like a father, has confused your mind. What is left to me in this world?"

Weeping, she turned away and went back along the path on which she had come.

"What can this mean?" growled Papageno. "Tamino sits there and doesn't move, and just lets the girl go. Where is my girl, my Papagena? All lies and deceit in this place!"

But what was this? A wizened little old woman appeared from behind the pillars and hobbled over to Papageno.

"Old woman, have you come to chase away my boredom?"

"Yes, my angel," the little woman replied in a croaking voice.

"A good idea!" said Papageno. "But tell me, how old are you and what is your name?"

"Your Papagena is eighteen years and two minutes old!"

"*M-m-my* Pa-pa-ge-na?"

"Yes, my angel. Don't you like me? That would be so sad for you. Then you would have to stay in this place and all your life you would get nothing but bread and water to satisfy your hunger and thirst... Think hard, my angel. That would be a pity, when we suit each other so well!"

Papageno was at a loss for an answer. After a time he said hesitantly: "Hm, yes, rather than grow old and gray on bread and water, better an old woman than none at all."

"See, my angel, now I am pleased with you," replied the little woman. "So I am getting not only a pretty but a clever man. Won't you give your Papagena a kiss, as sweethearts should?"

"Not so fast," Papageno retorted. "First I want to get away from here, and then we shall see."

Now the thunder rolled so loudly and terribly that Papageno nearly fell to the ground. This brought him to his senses at last. He took a hesitant step toward the old woman and next moment his eyes were popping with astonishment. The ugly little woman had changed into an enchanting young girl! Her dainty figure was clad in the most adorable feather dress, even brighter and more cheerful than Papageno's, and on her head she wore a cap of the same feathers. The new Papagena laughed mischievously at him.

Papageno: 'Tis love, they say, love on — — ly, that makes the world go round; I should not feel so lone - ly -, Had I a sweet - heart found, had I a sweet-heart found, had I — a — sweet - heart found.

Papageno hesitated no longer. He ran to her, intending to catch her passionately in his arms. But Papagena slipped out of reach like a bird, and for a royal bird-catcher that really was a humiliation! Before Papageno knew what was happening, Papagena had vanished from sight. So that was the punishment for his talkativeness. If I had only listened to Tamino, he thought sadly.

The prince had still not spoken a word. He was listening to the priest's chant, ringing out from the heart of the temple.

"O Isis and Osiris!"

The lofty invocation of the priests comforted Tamino and gave him new courage, although the thought of Pamina filled him with pain and compassion. How wretched she must be, believing herself betrayed and abandoned by her beloved!

But Tamino had no idea how desperate Pamina really was.

After taking her sad farewell of the prince, Pamina had nearly lost her reason. "O, gods!" she cried. "I cannot endure it! Here, with my wrathful mother's dagger, I will kill myself! Only in death shall I find peace!"

Pamina was about to plunge the dagger into her heart when

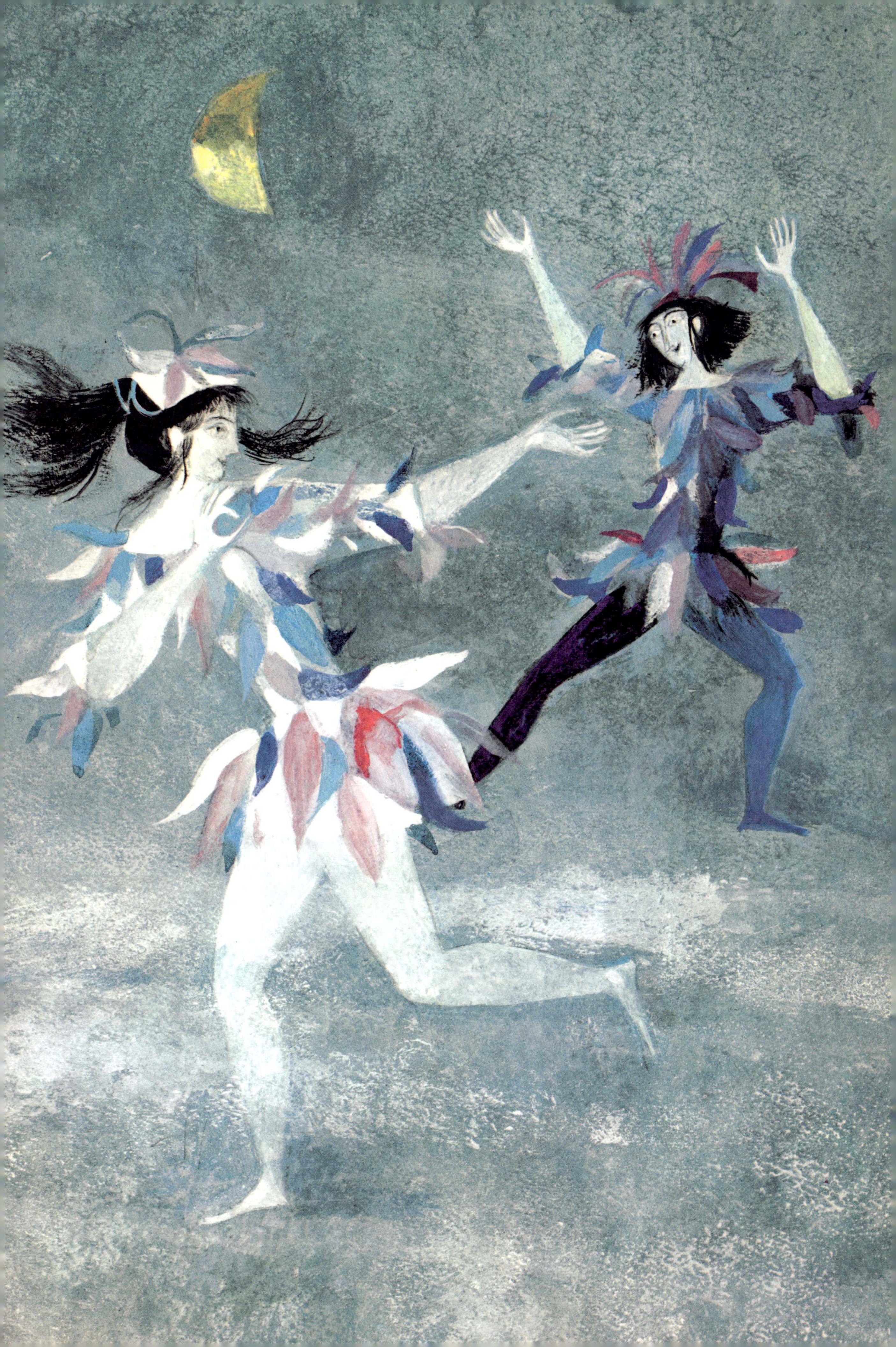

suddenly the three boys stood before her, hands raised in warning.

"Stop!" they cried. "You do not know what you are doing! Is this your reward for Tamino's faithful love?"

"Faithful love? Oh, do not mock me!" sobbed Pamina. "Tamino..."

"Tamino loves you," said the boys. "He is prepared to go through fire and water for you. If you are prepared to do the same for him, follow us."

"I am ready," said Pamina.

No sooner had she spoken than black night fell about her. The three boys could no longer be seen. Yet Pamina walked fearlessly forward into the darkness. Suddenly the sound of a tempest roared in her ears. Firelight glowed ahead of her, and as Pamina drew near she could see two mountains before her. Over one raged a waterfall, while the other spewed out flames. Through a cloud of boiling spray and showering sparks she recognized Tamino, who was led by two warriors clad in black.

The prince saw her too.

"Pamina in this place of terror!" he cried. "Now she can go with me no matter what happens, even if death awaits us. May I speak to her?" He turned to the two armed men.

"You may speak to her," they answered.

Now Tamino sped to Pamina through the spray and showers of fire and sparks.

"Pamina!"

"Tamino!"

Hand in hand they passed between the two mountains. Then the rushing water ebbed away, the fire was quenched, and a door opened before Tamino and Pamina. They stepped into a blaze of light and found themselves in Sarastro's Temple of the Sun, more beautiful than anything they had ever seen. Sarastro came down the white marble steps to meet them, followed by priests in ceremonial robes.

"Greetings," said Sarastro. "Your steadfastness, noble youth, has prevailed. Isis and Osiris, the gods of wisdom, have enlightened your mind. You have withstood the ordeal and won Pamina's hand and heart as your prize. And you, my child," he went on, turning to Pamina, "have proved that the evil spirit of your mother has no power over you. Your love has conquered night and death. Be happy with Tamino in my kingdom!"

Now the three boys led in Papageno. The gay feathers of his costume hung limply and had lost all their sheen.

"You, Papageno," Sarastro told him, "have not passed the test. Your simple mind made it impossible for you to keep your busy tongue in check. But you have a good heart; the gods absolve you from the punishment. See to it that you are happy with your Papagena!"

Papageno rang his silver glockenspiel. Then the girl in the feather dress ran out from behind the temple and came laughing toward Papageno.

"Papagena!"—"Papageno!" they cried together and as they hugged and kissed each other they danced round in a circle. "Papageno, Papagena! Papagena, Papageno!" they chirped as excitedly as two birds who have just learned to fly.

But all at once the sky darkened and amidst thunder and lightning the Queen of the Night approached with her three ladies and Monostatos. The Moor had shown her the secret way into the temple and now she was making her last attempt to destroy Sarastro's work. But even as the queen walked in the sacred place she felt her power dwindling.

"Back!" cried Sarastro. "Away from this place of peace! May your kingdom sink into eternal night!"

Once again the temple shook under a fearful clap of thunder. The earth opened and engulfed the queen and her train for all eternity.

From now on Sarastro's kingdom of the Sun was no longer threatened by evil powers. Tamino and Pamina lived happily by his side, protecting the treasure of wisdom and love to the end of their days.

But Papageno and Papagena returned to the forest and led a carefree life, as free as birds, in the natural kingdom of the gods.